THE CHOICE

BY TOI POTTS

BEAUTIFUL BLACK CAT
PUBLISHING

Speak for those who have no voice…..this book is
dedicated to all the babies yet to be born.

Love,

Ms. Toi

"How in the hell did I do this? What was I thinking? I wasn't thinking. Damn it!!" Zoe Clarkson couldn't understand how her world began to spiral into the mess that she was in. As she sat in her 10th-floor apartment overlooking Lake Michigan, Zoe fell on her face and cried as if her world was crashing down

and it was………

TABLE OF CONTENTS

THIS IS MY PLAYGROUND

My name is Zoe Clarkson and I'm a sister who knew
what she wanted in life and wasn't afraid to get it. This
is my story. A short story but one that needs to be
told. As a single mom, I knew what I wanted and
didn't want out of life. I was living the dream, my own
apartment with a great lake view, making more money
than I dreamed of, and a beautiful little human who
was the joy of my life. As life would have it, I wasn't
ready to settle down in a relationship and any man
who met me found that out quick. It was Friday and I
was out with my girlfriends having a good time at The
Lounge in the city when I turned around, and there
HE was, my Mister "I want that tonight" standing

about 20 feet away from me. I normally didn't approach men at The Lounge, but he caught my attention and I had to walk over and say hello. "Hello, and you are?" I said with the sweetest voice I could muster after several long island ice teas while trying to be gracious at the same time. My name is Quintus and you are, he answered? Quintus? Quintus? Who names their child Quintus? I thought to myself; before I got my words together. "My name is Zoe," I said with all the girl power in me. At this point I was looking up into those soft melting brown eyes and those L.L Cool J lips to die for, then he took my hand and we headed to the dance floor. We eventually closed the club down, Quintus walked me to my car and gave me his number to hook up in a few days. Of course, I made him wait a month before I called him and like most men I dated, he was waiting on my call. I liked being in control when it came to dating men, with less heartache and less drama. After clearing my schedule, Quintus and I were finally going out for dinner. I had my outfits on my bed just waiting for me to decide. Shall it be the "no small talk" let's get to business outfit or the "I want to be friends first" outfit? I really wanted tonight to be different, so the "I want to be friends" outfit was the one to wear. Dinner was perfect! We laughed and talked the whole time, this seemed to be the beginning of a wonderful friendship………… if only I could keep him out of my bed.

NOT ME! ARE YOU KIDDING ME?

It's been almost three years since our first dinner date,
and we have had our share of a whirlwind romance.
Quintus and I had remained "friends with benefits"
and my life, my life. I now have a beautiful daughter
living pretty well and just "doing me" to the fullest. I
remember that night like it was last night, the night I
went out to a party with Quintus……What the hell
was I thinking about going out with this man who was
only supposed to be my "side piece" when I wanted
it? Tonight, was different, I just wanted to dance,
drink and have some fun. Even though I ……….

Let me just stop right here! I wanted to give you, my readers a nice story of love, rejection, pain, and healing however

I GOT STUCK.

As I sit here in front of my computer early in the morning with tears in my eyes because I know I am supposed to tell you MY STORY. Yes, folks, Zoe Clarkson is me, Toi Potts and I do have a story to tell. One that may be just like yours or one that you may never need to live, who knows. This is how my story begins…… I had just moved to Chicago after surviving an abusive marriage and God had healed me from the scars and pain of that time in my life.

(PRAISE GOD I CAME OUT ALIVE) However, I

was not completely healed because a part of me just wanted to be free of everything and live how I wanted and that's just what I did. Late in 1992, I met a man who became my best friend. We met at a popular club in Chicago while I was coming off the dance floor. He asked me to dance and me being the lively, bubbly, person that I am could not resist. When I say we danced all night long…..we danced all night long. At that time, I wasn't in need of a serious relationship, I just wanted a friend and that is exactly what he was to me. We became the best of friends and I considered him my own personal Superman. Why Superman you ask? Well every time I needed a shoulder to cry on or an ear to listen to my endless talking, he would be there. I can honestly say we were friends.

As time went on, yours truly didn't want to be "just friends", I wanted more. What woman wouldn't want to be in an intimate relationship with her best friend(who was good-looking, smart, caring, and funny) so I did what any woman would do, I found a way to make it happen. (don't judge my life~lol) We began an intimate relationship and it wasn't all love, kisses, roses, and excitement. Our relationship was on and off for years which really made me want to kick myself in the butt for being so horny! Words of advice dear reader, if you have a friend and you two are great friends, don't cross that line unless he/she decides to make it official(Mr. and Mrs. official). Wait for it! During the time we were "on", it was him and me against the world. We were the envy of other couples because we genuinely loved each other. We were together more than apart, which explains how I became pregnant with our little human. It was during one of our off times, but I had a dilemma and called my Superman because someone was going to literally die that day. At that time in my life, there were some family members who played with my emotions one time too many. Seriously yall, I was premeditating the murder of several family members because I had enough of their games. Well, my Superman showed up and calmed me down, let me cuss, cry, and do what I needed to get through that time in my life. Yes, we were on again and life was great, until..........

After a moment of weakness and a night of pure passion, I woke up and all I could think was "Oh great, I'm pregnant". Women know their bodies and I really knew mine, that's why I went to the clinic to make sure what I felt was true. This was the time of truth for me and my friend because, in all honesty, I was not ready to have another child. My son was living in New York with his father and there was too much drama going on with that situation but what else could I do except having *this* baby. When I gave the news that we were going to be parents, his initial reaction was excitement, but I knew deep down inside I would be raising this child on my own. Peeps, I know them when I pick them, and I knew he wasn't going to be around like I wanted. Now don't start thinking "That man is a dog"!! He had issues just like me and situations going on in his life at that time as well and I really understood his position at that time…. He just wasn't ready.

In early spring, I gave birth to a beautiful, healthy little human who literally saved my life. (and the lives of some other people too) This little human brought a new meaning to my life and changed my world for the better. My life seemed to come into perspective when I held my bundle of hope in my arms, a new sense of life came over me like never before.

THE CHOICE

One would think everything in my life was going just fine and it was. I was living the life or so I thought. My Superman and I were off again as far as being in a relationship were concerned however something happened one day. I really couldn't tell you how we ended up seeing each other again or why we started dating again, I guess we needed each other and at that time, that was all that mattered.

We were "on" again and life was absolutely wonderful until that night, the night that we partied all night and came back to my place…. You know what happened and at the time my brain was not thinking clearly at all. Whirlwind romances can literally bring your life crashing down and it did. Few weeks later I didn't get

the visit from my monthly friend and I know

something was up because she would always visit on

time like clockwork. I made an appointment to see if

what my body was telling me was true and yes, *I WAS*

PREGNANT AGAIN! I couldn't think straight, my

little human was only a year and a half, I knew that I

would be raising both my children alone because my

Superman was just wasn't going to be there. What did

I do? I went to a friend in confidence (watch out who

is in your ear when making life-changing decisions)

who gave me their advice. During this time life

seemed to go so fast and I simply didn't know what

else to do. I told my child's father and his response

knocked me off my foot, he said "what am I going to

do?" What am *I* going to do? What the hell!!! I didn't

have sex with myself and produce a baby!! WTF!! I

was mad and made a choice that would alter my life

forever. I made sure my medical insurance from my

job would cover the procedure and it did. I told my

child's father what I wanted to do, and he had to come

with me since that was all he could do at that time.

I remember it like yesterday, on the day I made **THE

CHOICE,** I went to the clinic and there was a single

lady outside screaming MURDERER!!

MURDERER!!, I tried to ignore her, but those words

pissed me off because she didn't know me or why I

was making **THE CHOICE** all she wanted was to

condemn me. I went in and was determined to get

MY life back. I checked in and watched all these

women from every nationality, age, and background come in as I was completing my paperwork. As I went back to change and prepare for the one thing that I could never change, my mind was all over the place and I just wanted it to be over because I wanted my life back to normal.

THE CHOICE made me numb.

I didn't know what to feel. My life would never be the same because a part of my life was removed indefinitely and I couldn't get it back.

My unborn child was gone forever.

HEALING DOES COME

I sit here in front of my computer with tears rolling down my face like Niagra Falls because I feel the pain, rejection, and shame that comes when you have an abortion and make **THE CHOICE.** I know exactly how you feel if you've made **THE CHOICE** however, know that healing does come. I would be a fool not to tell you that it took years for healing to come because I was so broken on the inside because of **THE CHOICE** I made. I didn't think I could be forgiven because I took an innocent life so that I could live my best life. I must let you know how healing came for me and to be honest it is the only way you can be healed from the scars of abortion. What others don't tell you is that you will go through a grieving process for some time and that is not a pretty sight. You may also have medical complications in the future, that could prevent you from having more children. Also, you battle the feelings of guilt every day but there is hope. That hope comes from knowing Jesus Christ on a personal level. Hey, you've read this far, so keep reading…. I had to go back to the one man that loved me before **THE CHOICE** and loved me after **THE CHOICE**. He forgave me and restored the joy of living like never before and for that I am eternally grateful. You may be at the fork in the road of your life on the brink of making **THE CHOICE** and don't know what to do.

STOP AND THINK BEFORE MAKING THE CHOICE that will ultimately change your life forever and not in a good way. This book was written to help someone allow another little human being to enter this world and change it for the better.

You can make it!

You can love your unborn child more than you could imagine!

Your life will change but for the better!

Take a minute and pray. Ask God to help you and give you the strength to make the right CHOICE and give your unborn baby a chance at life with your help.

YOU ARE LOVED!

YOU CAN MAKE IT!

YOU ARE ACCEPTED BY GOD!

YOU ARE FORGIVEN & FORGIVE YOURSELF

YOU CAN DO THIS!

**YOU WILL MAKE THE RIGHT CHOICE
BECAUSE GOD CHOSE YOU TO BE THEIR
MOTHER!**

I am praying for you, my reader, that the love of God
will flood all over you and your little human today and
always.

Much love,

Toi

My CHOICE:

My CHOICE:

My CHOICE:

My CHOICE:

____

____

____

____

____

____

____

____

____

____

____

My CHOICE:

My CHOICE:

My CHOICE:

____

____

____

____

____

____

____

____

____

____

____